Table of Contents

FINRA and Investor Education

FINRA, the Financial Industry Regulatory Authority, is an independent, not-for-profit organization with a public mission: to protect America's investors by making sure the securities industry operates fairly and honestly. We do that by writing and enforcing rules governing the activities of nearly 4,500 brokerage firms with approximately 631,000 brokers; examining firms for compliance with those rules; fostering market transparency; and educating investors.

Our independent regulation plays a critical role in America's financial system—by enforcing high ethical standards, bringing the necessary resources and expertise to regulation and enhancing investor safeguards and market integrity—all at no cost to taxpayers.

FINRA's commitment to protect investors extends beyond strong enforcement. We believe that investor education is often the best form of investor protection. To that end, we provide free, unbiased education resources and tools to help investors evaluate investment products and professionals, and better understand the markets and the principles of investing.

www.finra.org

Smart Saving for College—Better Buy Degrees

If you have kids, you want a college education for them. But—

- Do you know how much college costs?
- Do you know how much you need to save?
- Do you know the many different tax-advantaged ways to save for college?

We've written this guide to answer these questions and give you the information you need to save and invest wisely for college. You can make a college education an affordable choice for you or your child.

College Costs Are Rising—Are You Keeping Pace?

According to The College Board®, the average increase in tuition and fees at public four-year colleges in 2011 was 8.3 percent for in-state students and 4.5 percent for out-of-state students.[1]

If college costs were to increase by 5 percent per year, in 10 years the cost of tuition and fees at a four-year private college would be $44,457, and the cost at a four-year public college would be $12,388. That's a four-year total of more than $177,000 for a private college and more than $49,000 for a public school—and this is just tuition and fees! For 2011, The College Board® reports that room and board charges average $10,089 at four-year private colleges and $8,887 at four-year public colleges.

But don't despair. While college costs are rising, many colleges still remain affordable. The College Board® reports that half of full-time students attending a four-year public or private nonprofit colleges pay $9,936 or less in tuition and fees.

So, college is still within reach for most families, but especially for those that start saving for it early.

1. *Trends in College Pricing 2011*, The College Board®.

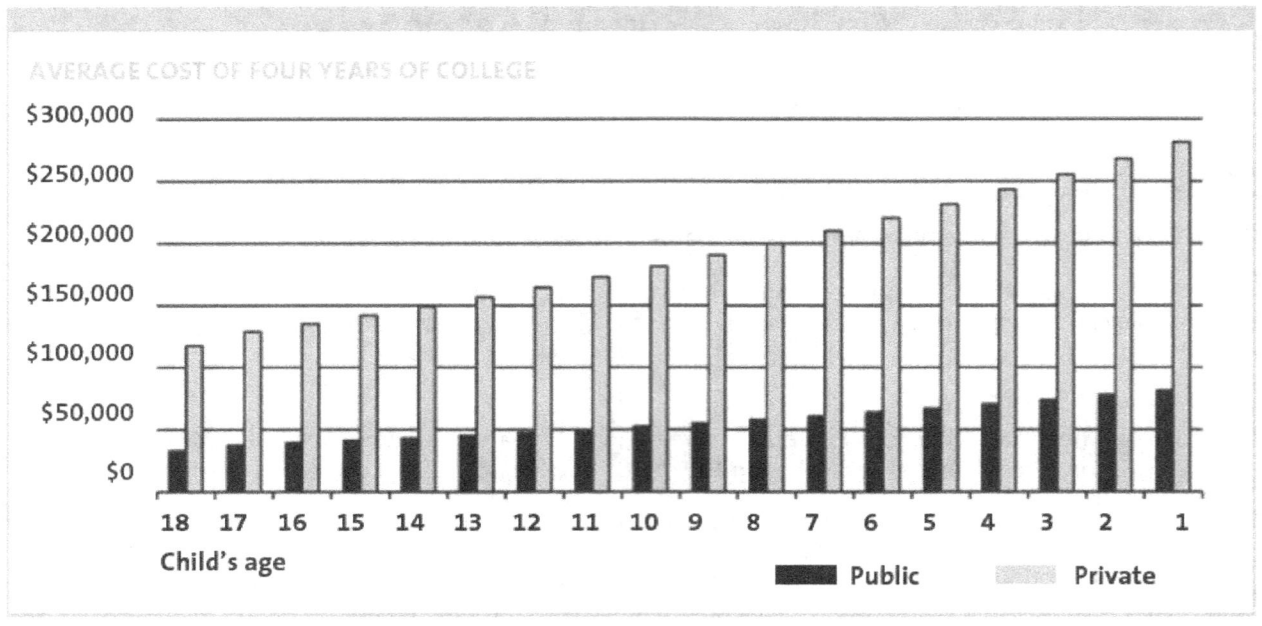

AVERAGE COST OF FOUR YEARS OF COLLEGE

Trends in College Pricing 2011, The College Board®. Assumes a 5 percent increase in college costs each year and a child entering college at age 18.

Saving for College with Compounding

Don't be daunted by the amount you may have to save. Small amounts of money, if invested early, can become sizable investments through the remarkable power of compounding. For example, if you save $200 a month at an 6 percent annual rate of return for your newborn child, you will have more than $76,000 for college when she turns 18. Use our College Savings Calculator to see how early and regular saving can make your money grow.

Saving for College Online Resources.

Use our College Savings Calculator to estimate the amount of money to invest each year to cover your child's college education. Remember to factor tuition, room, board and books into your calculation. If you know where you want your child to go to college, but don't know the current costs, you can use the National Center for Education Statistics' school locator to research the costs. If you are unsure where you want your child to go to college, The College Board® says a year at a private four-year college — for tuition, room and board — now averages $36,993, and the same year at a public four-year college averages $16,140.

► College Savings Calculator: *www.finra.org/college_calc*

► School Locator: *nces.ed.gov/globallocator*

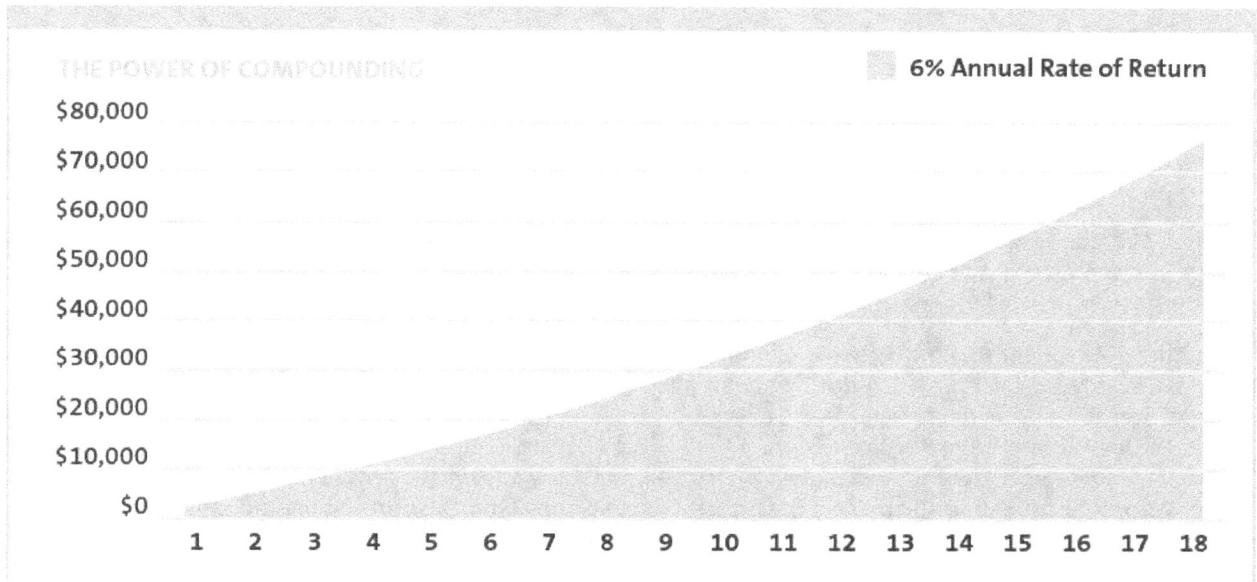

THE POWER OF COMPOUNDING   6% Annual Rate of Return

Don't Forget Financial Aid

As part of saving for college, you need to know whether your child will be eligible for financial aid, which reduces what you may need to save for college.

Be aware that saving for college might impact financial aid. Any investments or savings can affect federal financial aid eligibility. The impact on financial aid varies depending on whether the savings belong to the parent or the child. Savings in a parent's name can reduce federal financial aid eligibility by at most 5.64 percent, but assets saved in a child's name can reduce aid eligibility by as much as 20 percent. The good news is that 529 accounts owned by a child or set up as a custodial 529 account are treated at the lower 5.64 percent rate. States and private colleges may have their own rules for financial aid, and some states give more favorable treatment to pre-paid tuition plans and other college savings options.

Financial Aid Online Resources.

Financial aid is a complex and confusing area. To help students and parents navigate the landscape, the U.S. Department of Education's Office of Federal Student Aid launched Student Aid on the Web, a robust website that provides details on federal student aid programs, including grants, campus-based aid, work-study programs and loans. DOE also streamlined the process for applying for financial aid, enabling parents and students to submit the Free Application for Federal Student Aid (FAFSA) and monitor results online. The FAFSA website also features the FAFSA4caster tool, which estimates in advance how much aid your student could qualify for and how much the family might be expected to pay — referred to as the Expected Family Contribution (EFC). Another helpful website for understanding financial aid and determining eligibility is FinAid! The SmartStudent™ Guide to Financial Aid.

▶ Student Aid on the Web: *studentaid.ed.gov*   ▶ FinAid: *www.finaid.org*

▶ FAFSA: *fafsa.ed.gov*

Loans—Know the Cost

While savings may decrease the amount of financial aid you qualify for, you and your child will likely be in a much better financial situation on graduation day if you start saving for college now. The more you save now, the less you will need to borrow later. Yet for many students and their families, loans are a reality of higher education.

Loans are borrowed funds that must be paid back with interest (or paid back before interest begins to accrue). There are two broad categories of student loans—federal student loans, which are administered by the U.S. Department of Education, and private student loans, which are non-government loans issued by non-governmental lenders, including banks, credit unions and companies such as Sallie Mae.

While federal student loans have strict eligibility requirements and borrowing limits, they traditionally offer several advantages over private loans. For example, federal student loans charge a fixed rate of interest, and payments on principal typically are deferred until six months after the student graduates. Interest on federal student loans begins to accrue when the proceeds of the loan are disbursed to the school—but students who demonstrate financial need may be eligible for a subsidized federal student loan, meaning the government covers (or subsidizes) the interest as it accrues until the deferral period ends and you start repaying the loan. With unsubsidized federal student loans, borrowers can choose to pay the interest as it accrues or allow it to "capitalize." In other words, the interest rolls into the principal balance, compounding your overall debt. Capitalization can be costly in the long run because, when you begin repaying the loan, you start out with a higher principal balance—and so you wind up paying more in interest over the life of the loan.

In contrast to federal student loans, private student loans usually charge variable interest rates that are often higher than those available for federal loans. In addition, origination and disbursement fees can be high, interest accrues (and is often capitalized) during the student years and repayment options tend to be more limited and less flexible. For example, you might not be able to defer payment on a private loan if you decide to go to graduate school.

SMART TIP

Regardless of income, parents and students should research—and exhaust—federal student loan options before turning to private loans. Not all federal student loans are based on demonstrated financial need. Ultimately, if you apply for a federal student loan, you will need to complete a FAFSA form.

Additional Online Resources.

The best place to start looking for student loan information is on the U.S. Department of Education's Federal Student Aid and FAFSA websites, www.studentaid.ed.gov and www.fafsa.ed.gov. Two other helpful sites include The College Board Loan Center and the The Project on Student Debt, which works to increase public understanding of student debt and its implications for families, the economy and society.

▶ The College Board Loan Center: www.collegeboard.com
▶ The Project on Student Debt: www.projectonstudentdebt.org

Education Benefits for Servicemembers—Post-9/11 GI Bill

The Post-9/11 GI Bill pays for education and housing costs for military servicemembers and veterans who served at least 90 days of aggregate service on or after September 11, 2001, or who were discharged with a service-connected disability after 30 days. Eligible veterans can claim benefits for up to 15 years after leaving the military.

In addition to funding graduate and undergraduate studies, this newest version of the GI Bill covers on-the-job training, apprenticeship programs, flight schools and numerous other non-college degree programs. Benefits include:

- Tuition and fee reimbursement.
  - ▶ Effective August 1, 2011, all in-state tuition and fee charges are reimbursed at public institutions.
  - ▶ For private and foreign institutions, the tuition and fee reimbursement is capped at $17,500 per year, except for certain students attending private colleges and universities in the states of Arizona, Michigan, New Hampshire, New York, Pennsylvania, South Carolina and Texas.
  - ▶ Through the Yellow Ribbon Program, eligible veterans at participating schools may be able to obtain additional funds to help reimburse costs that exceed in-state tuition and fees.
- A stipend for books and supplies.
- A monthly housing allowance based on the Basic Allowance for Housing for an E-5 with dependents at the location of the school.
- Ability to transfer unused educational benefits to spouse and children.

Even if you aren't sure if you will use your Post-9/11 GI Bill benefits, it's a good idea to apply and lock in the benefits you are entitled to receive.

Online Resource for Servicemembers:

The Department of Veterans Affairs has a website devoted to educational benefits under the Post-9/11 GI Bill. In addition to information about coverage amounts for tuition, fees and housing, the site includes a road map to help determine which benefit is best for you, a benefits calculator that provides estimates for tuition, fees and monthly housing allowance, and a comparison chart of monetary benefits under the various GI Bills. The site also includes information about other education benefit programs administered by the VA. For specific questions related to educational assistance and the Post-9/11 GI Bill, call toll-free: (888) GiBILL-1.

▶ Post 9-11 GI Bill: www.gibill.va.gov

College Saving While Saving Taxes

Once you determine how much you need to save or can afford to save, you need to decide what types of college saving vehicles you want to use. In addition to mutual funds, regular brokerage accounts and bank savings accounts, there are now a number of tax-advantaged alternatives available to help you save for college. Get the facts about each of the options, and decide which type might be right for you:

- 529 plans
  - ▶ Prepaid tuition plans
  - ▶ College savings plans
- Coverdell Education Savings Accounts
- Custodial accounts
- Savings bonds

To help you understand the differences among these college savings options, use the College Savings Plan Comparison Chart on page 20. For additional help and information, see our Tips for Choosing College Savings Options starting on page 18.

Remember: The tax rules that apply to college savings options are complicated. Before investing, you may want to check with your tax adviser about the tax consequences of investing in any of these options.

529 Plans

Named after the section of the federal tax code that governs them, 529 plans are tax-advantaged programs that help families save for college. Selecting a plan requires homework. Every state offers at least one 529 plan and now a consortium of private colleges also offers a 529 plan. The tax advantages, investment options, restrictions and fees can vary a great deal.

Before buying a 529 plan, you should find out about the particular plan you are considering, and be sure you understand the plan's description of fees and expenses. Request an offering circular or official statement from the plan sponsor or your financial professional. Most 529 plans provide this document on their websites, where it may be called the "Disclosure Statement," the "Plan Disclosure Document" or something similar. You can find links to most 529 plan sites on The National Association of State Treasurers' College Savings Plans Network website, *www.collegesavings.org*, for information on the 529 plans you are interested in.

Two Types of 529 Plans

There are two types of 529 plans—prepaid tuition plans and college savings plans. Every state offers at least one of these types of plans. Some states offer both, and a consortium of private colleges also offers a prepaid tuition plan.

529 Prepaid Tuition Plans

Prepaid tuition plans allow parents, grandparents and others to prepay tuition at today's tuition rates at eligible public and private colleges or universities so that they don't have to worry about future tuition increases.

Contribution Limits

You pay for amounts of tuition (years, credits or units) in one lump sum or through installment payments. There are a number of options. Some prepaid tuition plans offer contracts for a two-year community college or a four-year undergraduate program, or a combination of the two, and can cover one to five years of tuition. Some plans even allow the contract to be applied to graduate school tuition.

Covered Educational Expenses

With only a few exceptions, however, most prepaid tuition plans do not cover other expenses, such as room and board. So you may want to consider other college savings options to cover these costs.

Guarantees and Safety Features

Most states guarantee that the funds you put into a prepaid plan will keep pace with tuition. Some states back their prepaid tuition plans by the full faith and credit of the state, meaning that if the program should find itself in financial difficulty, the state will step in to provide the necessary funding. Other states do not have a formal guarantee, but do have a formal process by which the state's legislature will consider making an appropriation if necessary. Some states offer no guarantees that the plan will fund the future cost of tuition or that the state will step in should the plan falter.

Residency Requirements and Other Limitations

Unlike college savings plans, most state prepaid tuition plans require either you or your child to be a resident of the state offering the plan when you apply. Some limit enrollment to a certain period each year. Many prepaid tuition plans also have age or grade limits for beneficiaries (*i.e.*, future college students).

Investment Options

Prepaid tuition plans have no investment options. Under prepaid plans, the price of the contract is determined prior to purchase and usually depends on the type of contract, the current grade of the beneficiary, the current and projected cost of tuition and the projected rate of return. These programs then pool the money and make long-range investments so that the earnings meet or exceed college tuition increases. When a child is ready to go to college, the plan transfers funds to cover the tuition directly to the institution.

Portability

If your child chooses not to attend a college covered by the prepaid tuition plan, all is not lost. Although you will not get the benefit of guaranteed tuition, all prepaid tuition plans allow you to use plan money to pay tuition at other colleges and universities. Many state prepaid tuition plans will pay out an amount equal to the weighted average tuition and mandatory fees at your state's public institutions, not to exceed the actual tuition and fees you incur. Most prepaid plans also let you transfer the plan to a child's brother or sister (although age restrictions may prevent transfers to an older sibling). Unfortunately, if your child chooses not to go to college and a sibling doesn't use the plan, or you need to cancel the prepaid plan, most plans will only give you back what you originally contributed with a reduction or elimination of any interest earned. Some plans also charge a cancellation fee.

529 College Savings Plans

With college savings plans, students of all ages can save for all college costs, including tuition, fees, room, board, textbooks and computers.

Not Limited to In-State Public Colleges or State Residents

Withdrawals from college savings plans can be used at most colleges and universities throughout the country, including graduate schools. Some foreign education institutions also may be eligible. Many states now offer at least one college savings plan that has no residency restrictions. You can live in Ohio, contribute to a plan in Maine, and send your child to college in California. However, if your state offers state tax advantages to residents who participate in the local plan, you'll miss out if you opt for another state's 529 plan.

Covered Education Expenses

College savings plans typically cover all "qualified education expenses" at eligible colleges, universities and other post-secondary institutions, including:

- Tuition
- Fees
- Books and supplies
- Equipment required by school
- Room and board

Contribution Limits

When you invest in a college savings plan, you pay money into an investment account on behalf of a designated beneficiary. Contributions can vary and are only limited by the maximum and minimum contribution limits set by most plans. Although the maximum contribution amount differs from state to state, in the majority of states offering college savings plans, the maximum amount that you can contribute for one beneficiary exceeds $200,000.

To further increase the amount of contributions you can make, you can open a second college savings plan in another state. Currently, the IRS only requires that contributions for one child cannot be more than the amount necessary for the qualified higher education expenses of that child. So if you want your child to go to an expensive college and graduate school, one option you have is to open more than one college savings plan.

Most states also offer very flexible minimum contribution limits. Many require a $250 initial contribution with subsequent contributions of as little as $50. These minimum contribution amounts can be reduced even further in many states if you make contributions through payroll deductions or automatic transfers from a bank account.

Not Just for Children.

If you are considering going back to college or graduate school, you can open a college savings plan for yourself. You will save on taxes, and if you end up not going to school, you can always transfer the money, tax-free, to another 529 plan for your children or spouse.

Investment Options

Typically, each plan gives you a number of investment options that allow you to invest in various mutual fund and exchange-traded fund portfolios. Some college savings plans offer age-based fund portfolios. When the child is younger, the portfolio typically invests mostly in stock funds, which carry a higher risk, but higher return potential. As your child grows older, the asset allocation becomes increasingly conservative as it gradually shifts to bond funds and other fixed-income funds.

Many states also offer non-age-based investment options, allowing you to select portfolios with conservative, moderate and aggressive asset allocations. Some states also offer investment options that allow you to invest in certificates of deposits whose interest rates are linked to an index that measures the average cost of college tuition.

Until recently, once you selected an investment option within a college savings plan, you could not change that option. Only new contributions could be invested in different investment options. The IRS now allows you to change your investment options once every calendar year in a college savings plan and when there is a change in designated beneficiary.

Investment Risk

Investing in college savings plans does come with some risk. Unlike prepaid tuition plans, they don't lock in tuition prices. Nor does the state back or guarantee the investments. There also is the risk with most college savings plan investment options that you may lose money, or your investment may not grow enough to pay for college. For example, if you choose a plan option that invests in stock mutual funds, chances are that your invested funds' annual performance will mirror the trends of the stock market. Thus, you may lose money during a declining market.

Fees, Charges and Expenses

All 529 plans have fees and expenses. Not only do these charges vary among 529 plans, but also they can vary within a single plan. Like mutual funds, a single college savings plan may offer more than one "class" of shares to investors. Often referred to as A, B or C classes, shares, units or fee structures, each class has different fees and expenses. You can look at the offering document to see if a particular college savings plan offers more than one class.

Higher fees and expenses can make a big difference in the value of your investment over time. Let's say you invest $10,000 in a college savings plan with a return of 8 percent before expenses. With a plan that had annual administration and operating expenses of 2 percent, after 18 years, you would end up with only $27,880. If the college savings plan had expenses of 0.65 percent, you would end up with $35,548—an additional $7,668.

529 Expense Analyzer:

Because plan fees and expenses can vary widely from plan to plan, we have developed an expense analyzer to help you compare how sales loads, management fees, underlying fund fees and other plan expenses can reduce returns.

▶ 529 Expense Analyzer: www.finra.org/529analyzer

Here's a list of some of the most common fees, charges and expenses found in college savings plans:

- **Enrollment Fee.** Many college savings plans do not charge an enrollment fee. Almost all enrollment fees are under $50.

- **Annual Maintenance Fee.** Most college savings plans charge annual maintenance fees. These fees usually range from $10 to $50. Many plans reduce or eliminate this fee for residents, if you make automatic contributions, or if you maintain a certain balance, typically $25,000.

- **Sales Charge (Front-End Sales Load).** Several college savings plans levy a sales charge when you buy certain investment options within a plan or purchase a plan through a broker or investment adviser instead of directly from the state. Generally, you can determine the sales load by looking at the fees and expenses section of the offering circular or prospectus. Not every plan has a sales load. In some plans, a sales charge may only be levied on certain share classes of the plan.

- **Deferred Sales Charge.** A deferred sales charge or contingent deferred sales charge (CDSC) is a charge you pay when you withdraw money from an investment option or college savings plan. It is sometimes referred to as the back-end load. The charge may start out at 2.5 percent for the first year, and get smaller each year after that until it reaches zero. Generally, you can determine the deferred sales charge by looking at the fees and expenses section of the offering circular or prospectus. Not every college savings plan has a deferred sales charge. In some plans, a deferred sales charge may only be levied on certain classes of the plan.

- **Administration/Management Fee.** This is the total annual college savings plan operating expenses expressed as a percentage of the plan's assets. For example, an expense ratio of 1 percent represents an annual charge to the plan's assets—including your proportional interest in those assets—of 1 percent per year.

- **Underlying Fund Expenses.** Because college savings plan portfolios typically invest in a number of mutual funds, they bear part of the fees and expenses of these underlying funds. This expense is expressed as a percentage of a mutual fund's assets. Because college savings plan investment portfolios sometimes invest in a number of mutual funds, the offering circular or prospectus may contain fund-expense percentages for each of these funds.

Get a Break on Front-End Sales Loads.

Like mutual funds, Class A shares of college savings plans often offer discounts that reduce the front-end sales loads you pay. The investment levels at which the discounts become available are called breakpoints. The amount of the discount is based on the size of your investment, and the discount increases as the size of your investment increases.

Prepaid Tuition Plan	College Savings Plan
Most plans allow you to prepay tuition at eligible public and private colleges and universities at today's price.	No lock on college costs.
All plans cover tuition and mandatory fees. A few plans allow you to purchase a room and board option, use excess tuition credits for other qualified expenses or cover all qualified education expenses.	Covers all "qualified higher education expenses," including: ▷ Tuition ▷ Room and board ▷ Mandatory fees ▷ Books, computers (if required)
Most plans set lump sum and installment payments prior to purchase based on age of beneficiary and number of college tuition years purchased.	Many plans have contribution limits in excess of $200,000.
Many state plans guaranteed or backed by state.	No state guarantee. Most investment options are subject to market risk. Your investment may make no profit or even decline in value.
Some state plans have age/grade limits for beneficiaries.	No age limit. Open to adults and children.
Most state plans require either plan owner or beneficiary to be a state resident at the enrollment time.	Most plans do not have a residency requirement. However, nonresidents may only be able to purchase some plans through financial advisers or brokers.
Most plans have limited enrollment period.	Enrollment open all year.

Common Features of Prepaid Tuition and College Savings Plans

Federal Tax Advantages

Among of the biggest advantages of 529 plans over other college savings options are the tax advantages they offer. In a 529 savings plan, earnings grow tax-deferred and withdrawals are tax-free when used for qualified education expenses. And both 529 prepaid plans and 529 savings plans allow for a gift tax advantage. Although the IRS typically allows you to give no more than $13,000 a year to another person without a federal gift tax, you can contribute up to $65,000 to a 529 plan in one year. A special tax law allows you to aggregate five years of the allowable $13,000 annual gift-tax exclusion to jump-start a 529 plan. While you will be precluded from making any further gifts for five years, compounding will make your earnings grow faster than if you invested $13,000 in each of the five years. Use our College Savings Calculator to see the difference in savings of using a lump sum to jump-start a 529 plan: *www.finra.org/ savings_calc.*

Also, anyone can contribute to a 529 plan. Unlike education savings accounts (ESAs) and saving bonds, which are discussed later, there are no income limitations. For most wealthy families, 529 plans are one of the few available tax-advantaged college savings options.

State Tax Advantages

State tax treatment of 529 plans varies from state to state. In 34 states and the District of Columbia, contributions are tax deductible if you're a resident of the state sponsoring the 529 plan. In five of those states—Arizona, Kansas, Maine, Missouri and Pennsylvania—you can claim a state tax deduction for any 529 plan, regardless of its location. The amounts you can deduct also vary. Colorado currently allows residents to deduct the entire amount of their contribution to their in-state plan for each beneficiary, up to the amount of their annual adjusted gross income. Rhode Island, on the other hand, allows only a $1,000 deduction in total for joint filers and $500 for single filers. Many states also follow the federal tax lead of allowing earnings to grow tax-free and imposing no state tax on qualified withdrawals from in-state and out-of-state plans.

A few states offer scholarships, grants or matching contributions for low- and moderate-income families. The Florida Prepaid College Foundation offers a limited number of needs-based scholarships and North Dakota offers a matching grant of up to $300 to participants meeting the state's income requirements. Go to *www.collegesavings.org* to compare plan benefits by state.

Control

Unlike custodial accounts and ESAs, 529 plans allow the account owner to maintain control over the assets in a 529 plan for the life of the account. You also can change beneficiaries to another "family member" of the original beneficiary. Thus, if your child gets a scholarship or decides not to go to college, you can name another beneficiary—even yourself. Some 529 plans, especially prepaid tuition plans, may limit or restrict your ability to change beneficiaries, so check the plan offering document.

Transfers

The assets of one 529 plan can be transferred tax-free to another 529 plan of another beneficiary, as long as the new beneficiary is a "family member" of the beneficiary of the 529 plan from which the transfer was made. "Family members" include, among others, the beneficiary's spouse, son, daughter, grandchild, niece, nephew and first cousin.

The assets of one 529 plan also can be transferred tax-free to another 529 plan for the same beneficiary. However, only one transfer of this type is allowed within any 12-month period. There also may be state tax implications when you transfer from one 529 plan to another. You may want to consult with your tax adviser before you make a transfer.

Withdrawals for Non-College Related Expenses

If your child decides not to go to college or you over-fund a 529 plan, you may pay a penalty in addition to any taxes you owe on earnings. If you withdraw money from a 529 plan that is not used for qualified education expenses, you are generally required to pay income tax and an additional 10-percent penalty on earnings.

There are a number of exceptions to this penalty. The penalty may be waived if your child gets a scholarship or is disabled. You also can avoid the taxes and penalties by transferring the 529 plan to another beneficiary who will use the funds for qualified education expenses. Furthermore, you can use our College Savings Calculator to estimate the amount you need to save so that you don't over-fund a 529 plan.

Coverdell Education Savings Accounts

Those who want more investment choices may want to consider Coverdell Education Saving Accounts (ESAs).

No Investment Restrictions

Formerly known as Education IRAs, ESAs are another tax-advantaged way to pay for college. Unlike 529 plans, your investment options are virtually limitless. Except for investing in life insurance contracts, you can buy and sell what you want whenever you want. Also, you can set them up at almost any brokerage firm, mutual-fund company or other financial institution.

Federal Tax Advantages

As with 529 plans, contributions are not deductible, but earnings in ESAs are tax-deferred, and withdrawals that are used for qualified education expenses are tax-free.

Education Expenses Covered

One advantage that ESAs have over other tax-advantaged saving options is that you can make tax-free withdrawals to pay for private elementary and high school expenses, as well as post-secondary school expenses. So if a private school is in the future, one option you might want to consider is saving for that expense in an ESA and using a 529 plan for college.

Sunset Provision

Unless Congress takes action, certain provisions of the Coverdell will expire at the end of 2012. Specifically, the current $2,000 contribution will fall to $500, and expenses for K-12 will no longer be allowed.

Contribution Limits

ESAs have two annual contribution limits for individuals:

1. You can give up to $2,000 to any one beneficiary assuming you meet the ESA income limits discussed below.

2. The total of all contributions to all ESAs set up for one beneficiary cannot exceed $2,000. If other family members set up ESAs for your child, you need to check with them to make sure this contribution limit is not exceeded.

If you exceed these contribution limits, there is a 6 percent excise tax each year on excess contributions.

Invest $2,000 a year at an annual yield of 6 percent from the time your child is born, and you will have a little more than $61,000 in college savings when your child turns 18. Can't save that much, or think you can get a higher return on your investment? Use our College Savings Calculator to estimate your savings.

Income Restrictions

A couple filing a joint return for tax year 2010* can contribute $2,000 if their modified adjusted gross income is less than $190,000 a year. The ability to contribute is phased out for couples filing jointly with modified adjusted gross incomes of between $190,000 and $220,000. Contributions are not allowed for couples filing jointly whose modified adjusted gross income is $220,000 or above.

Single taxpayers will be able to contribute $2,000 if their modified adjusted gross income is less than $95,000. Single taxpayers' ability to contribute is phased out if their modified adjusted gross income is between $95,000 and $110,000. No contributions are allowed if their modified adjusted gross income is $110,000 or above.

Organizations, such as corporations, can also contribute to ESAs and are not subject to any income limits.

Fees, Charges and Expenses

Fees, charges and expenses will vary depending on the investments you choose and the institution with which you open an ESA. Remember, however, that because of the fairly low contribution limits, even small annual fees or expenses could make a big difference in the value of your investment over time.

Figuring Your ESA Contribution Limit. If your Modified Adjusted Gross Income (MAGI) is between $190,000 and $220,000 (joint filers), or $95,000 and $110,000 (single filers), you can figure your ESA contribution limit by using the following equations:

Married Joint Filers

$$\$2,000 - \frac{(MAGI - \$190,000) \times \$2,000}{\$30,000} = \text{Contribution Limit}$$

Single Filers

$$\$2,000 - \frac{(MAGI - \$95,000) \times \$2,000}{\$15,000} = \text{Contribution Limit}$$

---

*See IRS Publication 970: Tax Benefits for Education for 2011 updates.

Custodial Accounts

Custodial accounts—Uniform Gift to Minors Act (UGMA) accounts or Uniform Transfer to Minors Act (UTMA) accounts—are another tax-advantaged way to save for college. A parent, grandparent or other adult is custodian for the account and makes all the investment decisions until the child for whom the account was opened reaches the age of majority. UGMA accounts are limited to money and securities. UTMA accounts can hold other types of property. You can set up these accounts at almost any brokerage firm, mutual fund company or other financial institution.

Advantages

In tax year 2010, for children younger than 18 or younger than 24 if a full-time student, the first $950 of unearned income is tax-free. The next $950 is taxed at the child's federal tax rate. Any earnings over $1,900 are taxed at the custodian's federal tax rate. To learn more about the tax rules for children, you should read *IRS Publication 929: Tax Rules for Children and Dependents*.

As with Education Savings Accounts, your investing options are virtually limitless. Nor are there any contribution or income limitations. In addition, withdrawals can be used for any purpose, not just qualified education expenses, without penalty.

Disadvantages

When your child reaches the age of majority—18 to 25 depending on the state in which you live—he or she takes control of the account and can use the money in the account for anything. Because you lose control over how the money may be spent, some parents and grandparents may not like this option. Another potential disadvantage is that because the account is considered the child's asset, it may have a bigger negative impact on future financial aid. Plus, you can't switch beneficiaries. If your child decides not go to college or gets a scholarship, you can't switch the money to a brother, sister or other family member.

Tax-Free Transfer to a 529 Plan. You now can transfer funds from a custodial account to a 529 plan if the plan accepts such transfers. However, you must liquidate any investments you have made in a custodial account because you can only transfer cash and pay taxes, if any, on any gains. Another problem with transferring custodial account funds is that the money is the child's asset, not yours, so you cannot transfer the 529 plan to another beneficiary. There also may be other restrictions and limitations.

Series EE and I Savings Bonds

U.S. Series EE savings bonds issued after 1989 or Series I saving bonds are another tax-advantaged way to save for college.

Advantages

Backed by the full faith and credit of the United States government, the interest from these bonds is tax-free if used for qualified higher education expenses. Also, interest on Series EE and I savings bonds is usually exempt from state and local taxes.

Disadvantages

For example, in tax year 2010* the full interest exclusion is only available to couples filing jointly with modified adjusted gross income of less than $105,100, and for single filers with modified adjusted gross income of less than $70,100. The interest exclusion is phased out if your modified adjusted gross income is between $105,100 and $135,100 for joint filers, and between $70,100 and $85,100 for single taxpayers. You can learn more about the Educational Savings Bond Program in *IRS Publication 970: Tax Benefits for Education.*

The rules for using savings bonds for education can be complicated. To learn more about using savings bonds for educational expenses, you can call the Federal Reserve toll-free at (866) 388-1776. You can call the Bureau of Public Debt toll-free at (800) 487-2663 for information on the latest rates for Series EE and Series I savings bonds, or at (800) 722-2678 to learn how to buy savings bonds directly from the federal government.

Savings Bond Online Resource

The Bureau of Public Debt's website also provides information on the latest rates for Series EE and Series I savings bonds and how to buy savings bonds directly from the federal government.

▶ *www.treasurydirect.gov*

*See IRS Publication 970 for 2011 updates.

College Tax Credits

The American Opportunity Tax Credit and Lifetime Learning Credit offer two ways to reduce your taxes while paying for college.

Ameican Opportunity Credit

This credit—which reduces the amount of income tax you may have to pay—is available for four years of college and can be used for course materials, in addition to tuition and fees. This credit equals 100 percent of the first $2,000 and 25 percent of the second $2,000, for a maximum credit of $2,500 per student. To qualify for the American Opportunity Credit, your child must be pursuing a degree, going to school at least half time and not have a felony drug conviction. The full credit is available to you in 2010* if your modified adjusted gross income is less than $90,000 ($180,000 for joint filers) with a phase out between $80,000 – $90,000 for single filers and $160,000 – $180,000 for joint filers.

Lifetime Learning Credit

With the Lifetime Learning Credit, you can claim up to 20 percent of the first $10,000 paid for college tuition and fees, for a maximum credit of $2,000 per tax return. Unlike the American Opportunity Tax Credit, there is no limit on the number of years you can claim the Lifetime Learning Credit. It may be used for under-graduate and graduate courses and even for tuition and fees when your child is attending school less than half time. But, you can only claim the credit once per tax return, no matter how many children you have enrolled in college at the same time.

The full credits are available to you in 2010* if your modified adjusted gross income is less than $60,000 if you are a single taxpayer, and $120,000 if you are married filing jointly. The credits phase out if your modified adjusted gross income is between $50,000 and $60,000 if you're a single taxpayer, and between $100,000 and $120,000 if you are married filing jointly. You can't get either of these credits if your modified adjusted gross income is $60,000 or above if you are a single taxpayer, $120,000 or above if you are married filing jointly or you are married filing separately.

If you qualify for an American Opportunity Credit or Lifetime Learning Credit, you can still claim the credit even if you make a withdrawal from a 529 plan or ESA. You just can't apply the credits based on qualified expenses paid with 529 or ESA money.

More information on the availability of these credits can be found in *IRS Publication 970: Tax Benefits for Education.*

*See IRS Publication 970 for 2011 updates.

Tips for Choosing College Savings Options

1. Understand the Tax Benefits

A number of college savings options offer tax-advantaged ways to save. Taking advantage of these savings options may greatly affect how much you can accumulate for your child's college education. In addition to the federal tax benefits of many college savings options, there may also be state tax benefits. Savings bonds are usually exempt from state and local taxes. Many states allow you to deduct some or all of your contributions to a 529 plan if you're a resident of the state sponsoring the plan. In addition, states may offer other tax advantages for 529 plans. Because of these state tax benefits, you might want to check out your own state's 529 plan before considering other plans.

Everyone's tax situation is different, and state and federal tax law can be complex. You may want to consult with your tax adviser about which college savings options are best for you.

2. Examine Fees and Expenses

All of the college savings options discussed above involve various fees and expenses. A college saving option with higher costs must perform better than a low-cost option to generate the same returns for you. Even small differences in fees and expenses can translate into a large difference over time.

While we explain the various expenses involved with many 529 plans, that does not mean that other college savings options don't have fees and expenses. If you invest in mutual funds through an ESA or custodial account, you should check the fee table in the prospectus to see how the costs of a mutual fund add up over time. If you invest in stock, make sure you understand how much in commissions you must pay and factor this into any gain you may make.

3. Know the Risks As Well As the Rewards of Your College Savings Options

Compared to saving for retirement, your college saving timeline is relatively short. At most, it may be 18 years. And for many people, it's a lot less. This can impact your ability to weather a market decline and increases your risk.

4. Understand Your College Savings Plan's Limitations and Restrictions

What happens to your college savings if your child decides not to go to college, you have another child or you lose your job? These events and many others could dramatically impact your college savings strategy. Unfortunately, most college savings options have various restrictions and limitations that may impact your ability to react to a changing situation. Review carefully any college saving options you're considering to make sure they have the flexibility and control you feel you need.

Our College Savings Plan Comparison Chart will help you understand and compare the various restrictions and limitations of each option.

Before investing in any college saving vehicle, carefully evaluate it and its investment options. Investment options with higher rates of return may take risks that are beyond your comfort level and are inconsistent with your goals. To learn more about the investment strategy of investment options you are considering and their risk, you should read the following materials:

- 529 Plans. Read the offering circular or prospectus. It usually contains the investment strategy and risks of a 529 plan and its investment portfolios. Most 529 plans provide this document on their websites.

- Mutual Funds. Read the prospectus and shareholder reports. Prospectus and shareholders reports are usually available from mutual fund companies or your financial professional. Mutual fund prospectuses also are available in the SEC's EDGAR database.

- Stocks and Other Securities. Read a company's registration statement or annual (Form 10-K) and quarterly (Form 10-Q) reports. These are typically available in the SEC's EDGAR database, *www.sec.gov/edgar.shtml*. For companies that don't file in EDGAR, call the SEC's Office of Investor Education and Advocacy at (202) 551-8090 to see whether the company has filed any documents with the SEC.

College Savings Plan Comparison Chart*

	529 College Savings Plan	529 Prepaid Tuition Plan
Ownership/Control	Contributor	Contributor
Investment Choices	Typically, plans provide several investment options.	None
Age Limits	None	Plan may set age or grade limits.
Expenses Covered Besides Tuition and Fees	Qualified education expenses for post-secondary education.	With a few exceptions, only tuition and mandatory fees for post-secondary education are covered.
Contribution Limit	Varies from plan to plan. Majority of plans permit total contributions in excess of $200,000 per beneficiary.	Fixed by terms of contract you purchase.
Federal Tax Advantages	Earnings grow tax-deferred and are tax-free if used for qualified education expenses. Option to consolidate five years of annual gift tax exclusions into one year.	Option to consolidate five years of annual gift tax exclusions into one year.
State Tax Advantages	Varies from state to state, but some states provide tax deduction for contributions, tax-free earnings growth and tax-free withdrawals for qualified education expenses.	Varies from state to state, but some states provide tax deduction for contributions, tax-free earnings growth and tax-free withdrawals for qualified education expenses.
Income Phase-Out	None	None
Penalties for Non-Qualified Withdrawals	Earnings are taxed as ordinary income and may be subject to a 10-percent penalty.	Earnings are taxed as ordinary income and may be subject to a 10-percent penalty.

Education Savings Account	Custodial Accounts	Savings Bonds
Contributor	Custodian until child reaches age of majority	Contributor
No restrictions	No restrictions	Savings bonds
Except for special needs children, no contributions can be made after a child reaches age 18, and withdrawals must be made before beneficiary reaches age 30.	Minor child	Owner must be at least 24 before the bond's issue date (not purchase date).
Qualified elementary and secondary education expenses or qualified higher education expenses.	No restrictions on types of expenses.	Tuition and mandatory fees for post-secondary and contributions to 529s and ESAs.

Contributor:
    $2,000 per beneficiary per year.
Beneficiary:
    $2,000, does not matter how many ESAs are set up.
	No limit	No limit

Earnings grow tax-deferred and are tax-free if used for qualified education expenses.	$950 in earnings are tax-free.	Interest grows tax-deferred and is tax-free if used for qualified education expenses.
None	None	Interest is usually tax-exempt from state and local taxes.
Single filers: $95,000 – $110,000 Joint filers: $190,000 – $220,000	None	Single filers: $70,100 – 85,100 Joint filers: $105,100 – 135,000
Withdrawals that exceed the beneficiary's education expenses for the year may be taxable.	None	Interest earned is taxed as income.

* Filing information as of 2010. See IRS Publication 970 for 2011 updates.

For More Information

Internal Revenue Service (IRS)

The IRS has information on the tax-advantage college savings options discussed here. *Publication 970: Tax Benefits for Education* is a good place to start. It discusses 529 plans, ESAs and savings bonds, as well as tax credits and deductions for higher education expenses. You can find other information on their website, *www.irs.gov*. You also can call the IRS toll-free at (800) 829-3676 to order publications.

College Savings Network

The National Association of State Treasurers' College Savings Plans Network website, *www.collegesavings.org*, provides information on 529 plans. Their site provides links to state 529 plan websites, information on state tax treatment and other useful information.

529 Plan Sponsors

Most 529 plans allow you to directly invest through them. They provide you with offering circulars and applications, as well as a wealth of information on saving for college.

Brokers, Financial Advisers and Mutual Fund Firms

Many brokers, financial advisers and mutual fund firms work with one or more 529 plan sponsors and have information and materials on 529 plans. Most of these firms can also provide you with information on setting up ESAs and Custodial Accounts. Many firms also have websites that can provide you with information on your college savings options.

FINRA

We have a Web page devoted to 529 plans. In addition, you can check if the firm or individual offering you a college saving option is registered with FINRA on our website, *www.finra.org*, or by calling our hotline at (800) 289-9999.

Bureau of Public Debt

The Bureau of Public Debt's website, *www.treasury direct.gov*, provides everything from educational information to calculators to a direct purchase program for savings bonds. You can also call the Bureau of Public Debt toll-free at (800) 487-2663 for information on the latest rates for Series EE and Series I savings bonds, or at (800) 722-2678 to learn how to buy savings bonds directly from the federal government.

FinAid! The SmartStudent Guide to Financial Aid

The Smart Student Guide to Financial Aid's Website, *www.finaid.org*, provides a lot of helpful information on financial aid.

Online Resources

You will also find a wealth of information about your various college savings options on the Internet.

529 Plan

A tax-advantaged investment program designed to help finance education expenses. There are two types of 529 plans: prepaid tuition plans and college savings plans. Every state offers at least one of these. Tax advantages, investment options, restrictions and fees can vary a great deal from one plan to another.

Administration/Management Fee (Expense Ratio)

Total annual college savings plan operating expenses, expressed as a percentage of the plan's assets.

An expense ratio of 1 percent represents an annual charge to the fund's net assets—including your proportional interest in those assets—of 1 percent every year.

Age-Based Fund Portfolios

College savings plan portfolios that change their asset allocation according to the beneficiary's age. Initially age-based portfolios invest primarily in stock funds. As the beneficiary grows older, the stock funds are replaced by more conservative investments such as bond funds.

American Opportunity Tax Credit

An educational tax credit designed to reduce education costs. This is an expanded version of the Hope Credit, available for four years of college and can be used for course materials, in addition to tuition and fees.

Annual Maintenance Fee

Total annual college savings plan upkeep expense. An annual charge of $10–$40 is a typical maintenance fee.

Annual Operating Expenses

The sum of all of a fund's annual expenses, expressed as a percentage of the plan's assets.

Annual Rate of Return

The rate of return on your investment, expressed as a percentage of the total amount invested.

Annual Report (Form 10-K)

Public companies are required to file an annual report with the Securities and Exchange Commission (SEC) detailing the preceding year's financial results and plans for the upcoming year. Its regulatory version is called "Form 10K." The report contains financial information concerning a company's assets, liabilities, earnings, profits and other year-end statistics. The annual report is also the most widely read shareholder communication. Form 10-Ks are available without charge on the SEC's EDGAR website.

Asset Allocation

A strategy for maximizing gains while minimizing risks in your investment portfolio. Asset allocation involves dividing your assets on a percentage basis among different broad categories of investments, including stocks, bonds and cash.

Beneficiary

The individual who receives, or may become eligible to receive, the benefits of a college savings plan.

Bond Funds

Mutual funds that invests in bonds. Some bond funds may focus primarily on short-term, intermediate-term and long-term maturities. Also known as fixed-investment funds.

College Savings Plans

This type of 529 plan allows you to invest in various mutual fund portfolios or other investments on a tax-deferred bases, and to pay college or graduate school expenses with tax-free withdrawals. Many states now offer at least one college savings plan that has no residency restrictions.

Glossary

Compounding

The process through which the value of an investment increases exponentially over time as interest or dividends are reinvested, so that additional interest or dividends are always paid based on the value of the initial investment plus the accumulated interest or dividends already received.

Contingent Deferred Sales Charge (CDSC)

A common type of deferred sales charge. The CDSC normally declines each year and is eliminated after a number of years.

Coverdell Education Savings Accounts (ESAs)

College savings plan in which contributions grow on a tax-deferred basis and withdrawals are tax-free if used to pay for a broad range of educational expenses, including private high school tuition. Unlike 529 plans, ESAs have annual contribution limits and income restrictions.

Custodial Accounts

Uniform Gift to Minors Act (UGMA) or Uniform Transfer to Minors Act (UTMA) accounts, created for the benefit of a child. An adult controls the funds until the child reaches the age of majority, at which point the account transfers into the child's name.

Custodian

The adult who has control over a custodial account.

Enrollment Fee

A fee assessed when you enroll in a college savings plan. Enrollment fees are typically between $10–$90 although some college savings plans offer free enrollment.

Exchange-Traded Fund (ETF)

A type of pooled investment. ETFs are baskets of securities that track a particular market index, such as the Standard and Poor's 500 Index.

Fixed-Income Funds

See Bond Funds.

Gift Tax

A tax assessed against a person who gives money or assets to another person without receiving fair compensation.

Hope Credit

An education tax credit designed to reduce education costs. Renamed the American Opportunity Tax Credit.

Lifetime Learning Credit

An education tax credit designed to reduce the costs of college education. It can only be claimed once per tax return regardless of the number of children you have enrolled in college at the same time.

Modified Adjusted Gross Income

Your annual adjusted gross income without taking into account any IRA deduction, student loan interest deduction, or certain other deductions as specified under the Internal Revenue Code.

Mutual Funds

Types of investment funds that raise money from shareholders to invest in a group of assets such as stocks, bonds, and money market funds. Mutual Funds often have a minimum investment amount and a series of fees associated with them.

Non-Age Based Investment Options

Any college savings plan portfolio that doesn't shift asset allocation according to the age of the beneficiary.

Non-Qualified Withdrawals

Withdrawals from a college savings account that are used for non-college related expenses. Non-qualified withdrawals are subject to income tax and an additional 10-percent penalty on earnings.

Pre-Paid Tuition Plans

This type of 529 plan allows parents, grandparents, and others to lock in today's tuition rates for a future student beneficiary at any of a state's eligible public colleges or universities, avoiding future tuition increases. There are usually residency requirements and no investment options.

Prospectus

Every mutual fund has a prospectus that provides information about the fund, as required by securities regulators. You can get a prospectus from the fund company (via website, phone or mail) or your financial adviser. Mutual fund prospectuses are available without charge on the SEC's EDGAR website.

Qualified Education Expenses

Approved expenses for college savings plans. All withdrawals from a college savings account that are used to pay qualified expenses are tax-free. These expenses include: tuition, fees, books and supplies, equipment, and room and board.

Qualified Withdrawals

Any withdrawals from a college savings account that are used at eligible schools for college-related expenses. These withdrawals are tax-free and cover expenses such as tuition, room and board, book and supplies, and other equipment intended for college use.

Quarterly Report (Form 10-Q)

A report that the SEC requires publicly held companies to file quarterly, that provides unaudited financial information and other selected material. Form 10-Qs are available without charge on the SEC's EDGAR website.

Registration Statement

A set of documents, including a prospectus, which must be filed with the Securities and Exchange Commission before a firm can release its initial public offering and begin trading.

Sales Charge (Front-End Load)

The fee charged when you purchase mutual fund shares. For example, suppose you want to spend $10,000 to purchase mutual fund shares, and the mutual fund imposes a front-end sales charge of 5 percent. You will be charged $500, and you will receive shares with a market value of $9,500. A mutual fund may offer you a discount if you:

- Want to make a large purchase.
- Already hold other mutual funds offered by the same fund family.
- Commit to regularly purchasing the mutual fund's shares.
- Have family members (or others with whom you may link according to fund rules) who hold funds in the same fund family.

You should ask your financial adviser whether these discounts or breakpoints are available to you. Not all mutual funds have a sales charge or load. Many mutual funds, called no-load funds, have no sales charge or load. You can find the sales charge in the fee table in the front of a fund's prospectus.

Stock Funds

Mutual funds that invest mainly in stocks. Some stock funds may focus primarily on smaller, mid-sized or larger corporations, or on specific market sectors. Also known as equity funds.

Tax Deductible

An expense that can be deducted from annually reported income to reduce the amount of tax payments to the government.

Tax-Deferred

Taxes that can be paid at a future date, typically when shares of certain investments are sold.

Tax-deferred mutual funds can increase interest payments because more money is compounded in the fund.

Glossary

Underlying Fund Expenses

Expenses or fees charged by an investment firm for managing funds for college savings plans. These fees come in addition to any administrative or management fees that a state government charges for running a college savings plan.

Uniform Gift to Minors Act (UGMA)

A tax-advantaged custodial account for college savings. An adult acts as the custodian for the account and makes all the investment decisions until the beneficiary reaches the age of majority. At that point the beneficiary controls the account and any assets in the account. UGMA accounts are limited to holding money and securities.

Uniform Transfer to Minors Act (UTMA)

A tax-advantaged custodial account for college savings. An adult acts as the custodian for the account and makes all the investment decisions until the beneficiary reaches the age of majority. These accounts are very similar to UGMA accounts, but in addition to money and securities, UTMA accounts can also hold real estate, fine art, and patents and royalties.

U.S. Series EE and I Savings Bonds

Backed by the full faith and credit of the United States government, U.S. government savings bonds offer a tax-advantaged way to save for college. The interest from these bonds is usually exempt from state and local taxes and is tax free if used for qualified higher education expenses.

FINRA INVESTOR INFORMATION

▷ **Obtain information on other investing topics**

Website: *www.finra.org/investor*
Phone: (202) 728-6964

FINRA BROKERCHECK

▷ **Check the background of a broker or brokerage firm**

Website: *www.finra.org/brokercheck*
Toll-free Number: (800) 289-9999

FINRA INVESTOR COMPLAINT CENTER

▷ **If you feel you have been treated unfairly**

FINRA Investor Complaint Center
9509 Key West Avenue
Rockville, MD 20850-3329

Website: *www.finra.org/complaint*
Fax: (866) 397-3290

FINRA DISPUTE RESOLUTION

▷ **If you seek to recover damages**

FINRA Dispute Resolution
One Liberty Plaza
165 Broadway, 27th Floor
New York, NY 10006

Website: *www.finra.org/ArbitrationMediation*
Phone: (212) 858-4400
Fax: (212) 858-4429

The U.S. Securities and Exchange Commission's Office of Investor Education and Advocacy has reviewed this publication. The SEC does not endorse any particular investment product, service, profession, professional or brokerage firm.